SQL SERVER

PERFORMANCE TUNING AND OPTIMIZATION

Declaration

I hereby declare that this document is based on my personal experience. To the best of my knowledge, this document does not contain any material that infringes the copyrights of any other individual or organization

About the Book

The purpose of this book is to make aware about what probable causes are & how to troubleshoot when we face any kind of SQL Server database performance issues. Performance tuning means to optimize the performance of SQL Server/ database/ instance by adjusting/ identifying the various bottlenecks causing degradation in database. If SQL Server instance/ database is not properly tuned or optimized, obviously we will face issues like slowness, bad performance of database which relatively affect performance of related application as well. So it's quite mandatory to have your database or SQL Server instance properly tuned to perform optimally. Whenever there is any database/ SQL Server performance issues, there might be various parameters/ factors included which might cause database/ SQL Server performance degradation.

Target Readers

This book is intended for all .Net Developers, Database Developers, Database Architects and Testers who are looking for a practical advice to solve SQL server performance issues in a database or web application.

Keywords

SQL Server Performance Tuning, SQL Server Tuning Tips, SQL Server Timeout issue, Performance Tuning Tips, Tuning Advisor, SQL Engine Tuning Advisor, Timeout expired, SQL Server Optimization.

Table of Contents

SQL Server Performance Tuning

The purpose of this book is to make aware about what probable causes are & how to troubleshoot when we face any kind of SQL Server database performance issues. Performance tuning means to optimize the performance of SQL Server/ database/ instance by adjusting/ identifying the various bottlenecks causing degradation in database. If SQL Server instance/ database is not properly tuned or optimized, obviously we will face issues like slowness, bad performance of database which relatively affect performance of related application as well. So it's quite mandatory to have you database or SQL Server instance properly tuned to perform optimally. Whenever there is any database/ SQL Server performance issues, there might be various parameters/ factors included which might cause database/ SQL Server performance degradation.

Factors involved in Performance Degradation

(1) The first factor involved in slow performance of SQL Server may be blocking on database/ SQL Server. Blocking is the basically the outcome of locks being issued against objects in a database. If a request is made against the same object with a lock issued against it, then a block occurs.

(2) There might be certain maintenance jobs like update statistics, backups or rebuild indexes running which might be consuming server resources & make databases/ SQL Server slow & degrading the performance.

(3) On Server side, there might be certain processes running on Server side causing high CPU utilization or Memory utilization

(4) Poor written queries – its most usual cause of poor performance. Poorly written queries or improper tuned queries may affect the database performance badly & may cause slowness.

(5) Space on databases i.e. log & data files disks can cause a serious concern to performance & may lead to unavailability of database as well.

(6) Memory configurations in SQL Servers – Min & max server configuration parameters must be properly set for improving the DB performance.

Identifying Bottlenecks

Analyzing Memory Usage

Memory is so important to SQL Server that not having enough will really strain your hard drives. Basically, anything SQL Server can't commit to memory for processing will be forwarded to the disk subsystem—for recording upcoming queries that need to be executed, and so on. Processing instructions from memory is much quicker than getting these instructions from the hard drive (virtual memory) and executing them. The goal is adequate memory and cache to handle everything your system needs. These counters provide clues for making sure that memory on your SQL server is sufficient:

- **SQL Server: Memory Manager: Memory Grants Pending.**

A memory grant allocates SQL Server a workspace in memory to perform queries. If this counter value is high, your SQL server is memory-constrained. A high value indicates that too many memory grants are in a queue, waiting to be carried out.

Often, large queries being executed by concurrent users will cause poor memory performance. Reducing the value of this counter increases memory performance. Look at improving your query performance, especially by converting hash-join queries to inner loop queries.

- **SQL Server: Memory Manager: Total Server Memory.**

This counter indicates how much dynamic memory SQL Server is consuming. The whole point of dynamic memory allocation is to give and take as needed; SQL Server is good at increasing dynamic memory usage, but not so well at decreasing it!

A good way to check whether this value becomes unusually high (and too quickly) is by stopping and restarting the SQL service. Record the initial value after restart, and then check it again after a couple of days. If the second value is significantly higher—say, more than double the initial value—SQL Server's dynamic memory-management process isn't giving memory back to the operating system as efficiently as it should. There may be a number of causes, such as not closing connections, or closing and destroying record set objects in your web applications' ASP/ASP.NET code using SQL Server. Until the service is restarted, dynamic memory is still being allocated to these connections and objects that are no longer used. Each time an application with poor coding practices is compiled and executed against a database, dynamic memory allocation literally becomes exponential.

- SQL Server: Cache Manager: Cache Hit Ratio. If this value is consistently lower than 80%, your system isn't using enough memory to fulfill cache requests for good performance, but rather is using the disk subsystem. Try allocating more memory to SQL Server or increasing system memory.

- Memory: Page Reads/Sec. This counter can tell you whether the system has an adequate amount of memory for SQL Server. Paging occurs when Windows has to use the hard disk (virtual memory) because no system RAM is available. If Windows is reading more than five pages per second from the paging file, that's excessive paging; you don't have enough system RAM for good SQL Server performance. Removing any unnecessary applications from the server, disabling any unnecessary services, and adding RAM should bring paging to a reasonable level.

Analyzing Processor Usage

Processor usage is very important to SQL Server because the more processor time available to execute instructions at any given time, the faster SQL Server can perform necessary tasks. Several factors can affect processor usage, from poorly designed databases and queries to increased disk usage. The following counters are good for checking up on the processor(s):

- **System: Processor Queue Length.**

This counter is good for clueing into processor strain. To come up with a good queue number for your benchmark, multiple the number of processors on your server by two. For example, if your server has two processors, a good queue length should not exceed four; if your processor queue length is consistently higher than four on a system with two processors, your CPU is bottlenecking, causing increased query-execution time. To remedy this problem, you'll have to tune queries, reduce paging, or come up with better indexes. If these steps don't improve queue length, it may be time to add another processor system.

- **System: Context Switches/Sec.**

SQL Server uses threads to execute batches of SQL statements from clients. If this value is high SQL Server and Windows are switching many times per second from executing on one thread to executing on another, increasing CPU time and bogging down the system. If this value is high, it usually also means that the queue length (see bullet above) is also high. To optimize threading and increase processor performance, try setting SQL Server to use lightweight pooling. Doing so will make SQL Server use fibers instead of threads. Fibers use fewer resources; when pooled, they also allow SQL Server to optimize processing time when executing SQL statements concurrently. Lightweight pooling is an advanced option and can be set to 1 (to turn it on) using the sp_configure system-stored procedure.

- Processor: %User Time and Processor: %Privileged Time. Viewing these two counters together is good for indicating unnecessary processor strain by handling excessive I/O requests to the disk subsystem. If the %Privileged Time is consistently over 20% and %User Time is consistently below 80%, you have excessive I/O requests. Check your disk counters to confirm this problem, and get your I/O requests to the disk subsystem down to a reasonable level (see the next section).

Analyzing Disk Usage

Increased disk time on your database server usually means that your system is using more virtual memory due to a lack of RAM (analyze memory issues as described earlier). Monitor these counters:

- Physical Disk: Avg. Disk Queue Length. This counter indicates how busy a drive is becoming due to excessive I/O requests. If one drive is getting much more activity than another, try moving some SQL Server files from the busy drive(s) to other drives that are not so busy. This technique will help to spread the disk I/O activity and reduce bottlenecking on one drive.

- SQL Server: Databases: Log Flush Wait Time and SQL Server: Databases: Log Flush Waits/Sec. Disk I/O performance becomes especially important when SQL Server writes a transaction to the transaction log on the hard drive. The busier your databases are, the more disk I/O time will increase. These two counters tell you whether your disk I/O performance is sufficient for handling transaction log requests. The greater the wait time, the longer SQL Server is waiting to write the next transaction to the disk subsystem. As your server gets busier, these values increase because there are more sequential writes to the log. Make sure that I/O performance is sufficient by keeping these numbers reasonable under peak conditions.

Monitoring processes running on a server

Following query can be run to check all processes running on a server.

SELECT p.SPID, Blocked_By = p.Blocked, p.Status, p.LogiName, p.HostName, Program = coalesce('Job: ' + j.name, p.program_name), DBName = db_name(p.dbid), Command = p.cmd, CPUTime = p.cpu, DiskIO = p.physical_io, LastBatch = p.Last_Batch, LastQuery = coalesce((select [text] from sys.dm_exec_sql_text(p.sql_handle)),''), p.WaitTime, p.LastWaitType, LoginTime = p.Login_Time, RunDate = GetDate(), [Server] = serverproperty('machinename'), [Duration(s)] = datediff(second, p.last_batch, getdate()) FROM master..sysprocesses p left outer join msdb.dbo.sysjobs j on substring(p.program_name,32,32) = substring(sys.fn_varbintohexstr(j.job_id),3,100) where p.spid > 50 and p.status <> 'sleeping' and p.spid <> @@spid order by p.spid

Following observations can be made from the query result:

a. Deadlock: Blocked_By can be checked to find out if deadlock is happened.
b. Resource Utilization: In case CPUTime and/or DISKIO of a process is more for a long time, it can cause issue around performance of rest all processes running on the server.
c. Status Tracking: In case the process takes longer to execute, the wait_time & LastWaitType can be checked to see if the process is waiting and as per the LastWaitType, appropriate action can be taken.

How queries are executed

1. Parsing is a step during which syntax of the statement is validated and clauses are converted into internal compiler structures. Execution tree is produced here.

2. Execution tree is a structure that describes the logical steps needed to transform the source data into the format required by the result set.

3. Normalization is a step during which objects are verified, views are replaced with their definitions and implicit type conversions are performed.

4. Optimization is a most important step, during which execution plan is formed.

5. Execution plans are reused and cached in memory. If SQL query engine finds a suitable execution plan that is already cached, it will use it. By the same time, "expired" execution plans are removed from cache.

6. After that, execution plan is cached in a specially allocated buffer called procedure cache.

7. After that, the relational engine begins executing the execution plan. If any metadata is required from the base table. Relation engine uses the OLEDB connection so that storage engine pass up the data from the row set requested from the relation engine.

Comparison between Stored Procedure and Raw SQL

Stored Procedure:

1. Execution Plan is cached.

2. Not possible to inject SQL. (Unless dynamic SQL used inside).

3. Better Security isolation. (ownership chain concept)

4. Need to recompile from time to time as data changes.

Raw SQL:

1. Compiled every time (more memory in procedure cache).

2. Possible to inject SQL.

3. No security isolation.

Common causes of poor SQL Server performance

1. Poorly written queries and database schema
   - Unnecessary joins.
   - Unnecessary ORDER BY clauses.
   - Missing indexes.

2. Long running queries(blocking and deadlock)
   - Long running transactions.
   - Bulky insert or updates.

3. Memory Pressure
   - Those pages that are accessed frequently cannot fit into the SQL server memory which causes more disk I/O.
4. Poor Disk Performance
   - Disk fragmentation of database files (external fragmentation).
   - Index and data pages fragmentation within database files (internal fragmentation)

Execution Plan

1. SQL query execution Plan is a detailed strategy as determined by SQL query optimizer: cost-based optimizer.
2. Generation of Optimal execution Plan is most important step of query execution.
3. Execution Plan includes:
   - Which indexes should be used?
   - How to perform JOIN operations?
   - How to order and group resulting data?
   - In what order tables should be processed?
   - If cached data and previously compiled plans can be reused?
4. Lowest cost-based decision Tree.
5. Provides Fast results.

SQL Server Query Execution Plan Analysis

When it comes time to analyze the performance of a specific query, one of the best methods is to view the query execution plan. A query execution plan outlines how the SQL Server query optimizer actually ran (or will run) a specific query. This information is very valuable while analyzing the reason for slow performance of a specific query.

Viewing Query Execution Plan

Different ways to view a query's execution plan:

Using Query Analyzer

- From within Query Analyzer is an option called "Show Execution Plan" (located on the Query drop-down menu). If this option is on, then whenever a query is run in Query Analyzer, a query execution plan (in graphical format) is displayed in a separate window.
- If we want to see an execution plan, without running the query, choose the option "Display Estimated Execution Plan" (located on the Query drop-down menu). When this option is selected, immediately an execution plan (in graphical format) will appear. The difference between these two (if any) is accountable to the fact that when a query is really run (not simulated, as in this option), current operations of the server are also considered. In most cases, plans created by either method will produce similar results. This method won't work for stored procedures containing temporary tables.
- From within Query Analyzer, the command SET SHOWPLAN_TEXT ON can be run. Once this command is run, any query that is executed in this Query Analyzer sessions will not be run, but a text-based version of the query plan will be displayed. If the query being run uses temp tables, then the command, SET STATISTICS PROFILE ON must be run before running the query.

Using Profiler

- While creating a SQL Server Profiler trace, one of the events that should be collect is called: MISC: Execution Plan. This information (in text form) shows the execution plan used by the query optimizer to execute the query.

Potential performance Bottlenecks

- Index or table scans: May indicate a need for better or additional indexes.
- Bookmark Lookups: Consider changing the current clustered index, consider using a covering index, and limit the number of columns in the SELECT statement.
- Filter: Remove any functions in the WHERE clause, don't include Views in your Transact-SQL code, may need additional indexes.
- Sort: Does the data really need to be sorted? Can an index be used to avoid sorting? Can sorting be done at the client more efficiently?

It is not always possible to avoid these, but the more you can avoid them, the faster your performance will be.

Using Query Analyzer

Reading Graphical Query Execution Plan

- In very complex query plans, the plan is divided into many parts, with each part, listed one on top of the other on the screen. Each part represents a separate process or step that the query optimizer had (has) to perform in order to get to the final results.
- Each of the execution plan steps is often broken down into smaller sub-steps. Unfortunately, we don't view the sub-steps from left to right, but from right to left. This means we must scroll to the far right of the graphical query plan to see where each step starts.
- Each of the sub-steps and steps is connected by an arrow, showing the path (order) taken of the query when it was executed.
- Eventually, all of the parts come together at the top left side of the screen.
- If cursor is moved above any of the steps or sub-steps, a pop-up window is displayed, providing more detailed information about this particular step or sub-step.
- If cursor is moved over any of the arrows connecting the steps and sub-steps, a pop-up window comes up, showing how many records are being moved from one step or sub-step to another step or sub-step.

Interpreting Graphical Query Execution Plan in Detail

1. Arrows

The arrows that connect one icon to another in a graphical query plan have different thicknesses. The **thickness of the arrow** indicates the relative cost in the number of rows and row size of the data moving between each icon. The thicker the arrow, the more the relative cost is. These indicate what is happening within the query plan of query. For example, thick lines should be at the right of the graphical execution plan, not the left. If they are on the left, this could indicate that too many rows are being returned, and that the query execution plan is less than optimal.

2. Percentage Cost

In an execution plan, each part of it is assigned a percentage cost. This represents how much this part costs in regard to resource use, relative to the rest of the execution plan. While analyzing an execution plan, the focus should be on those parts that have the largest percentage cost. This way, limited time is used in focusing on those areas that have the greatest potential for a return on time invested.

3. Multiple executions

In an execution plan, some parts of the plan are executed more than once. Any part that takes more than one execution should be analyzed closely, and it should be seen if there is any way to reduce the number of executions performed. The fewer executions that are performed, the faster the query will be executed.

4. I/O and CPU Cost

These figures are used by the Query Optimizer to help it make the best decision. Smaller I/O or CPU cost uses less server resources than a higher I/O or CPU cost.

5. Indexes

One of the more useful things while examining an execution plan to look for is how indexes were used (if at all) by the query optimizer to retrieve data from tables from a given query. By finding out if an index was used, and how it was used, it can be determined if the current indexes are allowing the query to run as well as it possibly can.

When the cursor is placed over a table name (and its icon) in a graphical execution plan, and display the pop-up window, several messages come up. These messages tell if and how an index was used to retrieve data from a table. They include:

- **Table Scan**

  This means there was no clustered index on the table and that no index was used to look up the results. Literally, each row in the table being queried had to be examined. If a table is relatively small, table scans can be very fast, sometimes faster than using an index but on large tables, indexes should be used. If the amount of data to be retrieved is large, relative to the size of the table, or if the data is not selective (which means that there are many rows with the same values in the same column), a table scan is often performed instead of an index seek because it is faster. For example, if a table has 10,000 rows, and the query returns 1,000 of them, then a table scan of a table with no clustered index will be faster than trying to use a non-clustered index.

- **Estimated Row Count**

  While viewing the pop-up window, move the cursor over a table in a graphical query plan, notice the "Estimated Row Count" number. This number is the query optimizer's best guess on how many rows will be retrieved. If a table scan was done, and this number is very high, this tells that the table scan was done because a high number of records were returned, and that the query optimizer believed that it was faster to perform a table scan than use the available non-clustered index.

- **Index Seek**: This means that the query optimizer used a non-clustered index on the table to look up the results. Performance is generally very quick, especially when few rows are returned.
- **Clustered Index Seek**: This means that the query optimizer was able to use a clustered index on the table to look up the results, and performance is very quick. This is the fastest type of index lookup SQL Server can do.
- **Clustered Index Scan**: A clustered index scan is like a table scan, except that it is done on a table that has a clustered index. Like a regular table scan, a clustered index scan may indicate a performance problem. Generally, they occur for two different reasons.
  - There may be too many rows to retrieve, relative to the total number of rows in the table. See the "Estimated Row Count" to verify this.
  - It may be due to the column queried in the WHERE clause may not be selective enough. In any event, a clustered index is generally faster than a standard table scan, as not all records in the table always have to be searched when a clustered index scan is run, unlike a standard table scan.

Generally, the only thing that can be done to change a clustered index scan to a clustered index seek is to rewrite the query so that it is more restrictive and fewer rows are returned.

6. Joins

In most cases, the query optimizer will analyze joins and JOIN the tables using the most efficient join type, and in the most efficient order. But not always. In the graphical query plan, icons representing the different types of JOINs used in the query can be seen. In addition, each of the JOIN icons will have two arrows pointing to it. The upper arrow pointing to the JOIN icon represents the outer table in the join, and the lower arrow pointing to the JOIN icon represent the inner table in the join. Follow the arrows back to see the name of the table being joined.

Place the cursor over the arrows pointing to the upper and lower JOINs, a popup window showing how many rows are being sent to the JOIN for processing will come up. The upper arrow should always have fewer rows than the lower arrow. If not, then the JOIN order selected by the query optimizer might be incorrect.

First of all, let's look at JOIN types. SQL Server can JOIN a table using three different techniques:

1. Nested loop: Fastest one but not always feasible
2. Hash Join: Slower than Nested join
3. Merge Join: Slower than Nested join generally but when very large tables are joined, a merge join may be the best option. The only way to know is to try both and see which one is the most efficient.

If a particular query is slow, it may be because the JOIN type is not the optimum one for the data, then joins can be made to override the query optimizer's choice by using a JOIN hint.

Join Hints:

Join order is also selected by the query optimizer, which it trying to select the most efficient order to JOIN tables. For example, for a nested loop join, the upper table should be the smaller of the two tables. For hash joins, the same is true; the upper table should be the smaller of the two tables. If the query optimizer is selecting the wrong order, it can be overridden using JOIN hints.

In many cases, the only way to know for sure if using a JOIN hint to change JOIN type or JOIN order will boost or hinder performance is to give them a try and see what happens.

Note: For more details on Join Hints SQL Server Books Online

7. Parallelism

If SQL Server has multiple CPUs, and the default setting in SQL Server have not been changed to limit SQL Server's ability to use all of the CPUs in the server, then the **query optimizer will consider using parallelism** to execute some queries. Parallelism refers to the ability to execute a query on more than one CPU at the same time. In many cases, a query that runs on multiple processors is faster than a query that only runs on a single processor, but not always.

The Query Optimizer will not always use parallelism, even though it potentially can. This is because the Query Optimizer takes a variety of different things into consideration before it decides to use parallelism. For example, how many active concurrent connections are there, how busy is the CPU, is there enough available memory to run parallel queries, how many rows are being processed, and what is the type of query being run? Once the Query Optimizer collects all the facts, then it decides if parallelism is best for this particular run of the query. In some cases, the overhead of using multiple processors is greater than the resource savings of using them. While the query processor does try to weigh the pros and cons of using a parallel query, it doesn't always guess correctly.

If parallelism seems to be hurting the performance of a particular query, it can be turned off for that particular query by using the OPTION (MAXDOP 1) hint.

The only way to know for sure is to test the query both ways, and see what happens

8. Red colored icon

If the text of an icon is displayed in **red**, not black, which is the normal color, it means that the related table is missing some statistics that the Query Optimizer would like to have in order to come up with a better execution plan.

To create the missing statistics, right-click on the icon and select "Create Missing Statistics". This will display the "Create Missing Statistics" dialog box, where you can then easily add the missing statistics.

If an option to update missing statistics comes up, it should always be done as it will most likely benefit the performance of the query that is being analyzed.

9. Icon labeled "Assert"

Sometimes, when viewing a graphical query execution plan, you see an icon labeled "Assert." All this means is that the query optimizer is verifying a referential integrity or check constraint to see if the query will violate it or not. If not, there is no problem. But if it does, then the Query Optimizer will be unable to create an execution plan for the query and an error will be generated.

10. Bookmark Lookup

"Bookmark lookups are quite common to see. They tell that the Query Processor had to look up the row columns it needs from the table or a clustered index, instead of being able to read it directly from a non-clustered index.

For example, if all of the columns in the SELECT, JOIN, and WHERE clauses of a query don't all exist in the non-clustered index used to locate the rows that meet the query's criteria, then the Query Optimizer has to do extra work and look at the table or clustered index to find all the columns it needs to satisfy the query.

Another cause of a bookmark lookup is using SELECT *, which should never be used.

Bookmark lookups are not ideal from a performance perspective because extra I/O is required to look up all the columns for the rows to be returned.

Ways to avoid bookmark Lookups are:

1. Create a clustered index that will be used by the WHERE clause
2. Create a covering non-clustered index,
3. Create an indexed view

11. Temporary table in tempdb database

Sometimes, the Query Optimizer will need to create a temporary worktable in the tempdb database. If this is the case, it will be indicated in the graphical query execution plan with an icon labeled like one of the following:

- Index Spool
- Row Count Spool
- Table Spool.

Anytime that a work table is used, the performance is generally hurt because of the extra I/O generated while maintaining a worktable. Ideally, there should be no worktables. Unfortunately, they cannot always be avoided. And sometimes their use can actually boost performance because using a worktable is more efficient that the alternatives.

Take a careful look at such a query and see if there is anyway it can be rewritten to avoid the work table. There may not be.

12: Stream Aggregate icon

If Stream Aggregate icon comes up, this means is that some sort of aggregation into a single input is being performed. This is most commonly seen when a DISTINCT clause is used, or any aggregation operator, such as AVG, COUNT, MAX, MIN, or SUM.

Using Profiler to Analyze Query Execution Plan

One of the advantages of using Profiler instead of Query Analyzer to display execution plans is that it can do so for a great many queries from your actual production work, instead of running one at a time using Query Analyzer.

To capture and display query execution plans using Profiler, you must create a trace using the following configuration:

Events to Capture

- Performance: Execution Plan
- Performance: Show Plan All
- Performance: Show Plan Statistics
- Performance: Show Plan Text

Data Columns to Display

- StartTime
- Duration
- TextData
- CPU
- Reads
- Writes

Filters

- Duration. You will want to specify a maximum duration, such as 5 seconds, so that you don't get flooded with too much data.

    Note: This is only a guideline; more information can captured in trace.

If **OPTION FAST** hint is used in a query, the Execution Plan results may not be what you expect. The Execution Plan that is displayed is based on the results of using the FAST hint, not the actual Execution Plan for the full query.

The FAST hint is used to tell the Query Optimizer to return the specified number of rows as fast as possible, even if they hurts the overall performance of the query. The purpose of this hint is to return a specified number of records quickly in order to produce an illusion of speed for the user. Once the specified number of rows is returned, the remaining rows are retuned as they would be normally.

So if FAST hint is used, the execution plan will be for only those rows that are returned FAST, not for all of the rows.

Joins Strategy

The characteristics of the three physical join operators can be summarized as follows:

- Nested Loop Join: This is preferred where the inputs are relatively small and the inner table involved in the join has an index.

  Hash Join: It supports data warehousing queries involving medium to large inputs.

  Merge Join: This is preferred when the inputs are medium/ large, having indexes and
  If the output must be in an order.

- Nested Loop joins supports large number of concurrent users while Hash join does not. Merge join involving many-to-one join only supports large number of concurrent users.

- Nested Loop join does not require any memory while Hash join requires memory as it creates a hash table for its use. Merge join may require memory for sorting purpose if the two inputs are not in sorted order.

- Merge and Hash join expects the inputs to be in sorted order while Nested Loop join does not.

Optimization Techniques

Optimizing SQL Clause

SARG-able Where Clause.

a. SARG= Searchable ARGument (Creating SARG-able Where Clause is one of the most important part of Performance Tuning).
b. It Limits the Search because it specifies an exact match, a range of values, or combination of two or more SARG values joined by AND Clause.
c. SARG-able Operators contains (=,>, <,>=, <=, BETWEEN and LIKE).
d. These are not SARG-able Operators such as NOT,! =, <>, NOT EXISTS, NOT IN and NOT LIKE.

Avoid implicit convert.

a. It Generally Occurs When SQL SERVER encounters WHERE Clause containing comparison of different Data Types then it performs an implicit CONVERT operation.
b. It slows down Query Execution thus requires more Resources and hence increasing Execution cost.
c. It should be remove by adjusting data types of Parameters. (If required better to do it explicitly by declaring local variable of correct type. After that Local variable can be used in SARG –able WHERE clause)

Avoid unnecessary ORDER BY

a. ORDER BY Clause makes the SQL SEVER to sort Result set

b. SQL SERVER try to use index to perform sorting.

c. IF SQL SERVER already have an index to retrieve the data specified in WHERE clause, no additional cost is incurred by ORDERBY –data in the index is already in sorted manner.
d. IF SQL SERVER does not have index to use for ORDER BY, It will use the memory to sort the data. Or it will use the tempdb to store temporarily result set, if there is more data to sort. Hence negatively impact on Performance.

Optimizing Database Schema

Indices and statistics.

    a. Index in SQL SERER is a B-Tree Structure for storing Key Values.

    b. SQL SERVER maintains Statistics in addition to Index that describes how many records are expected to be found in an index.

    c. During query Optimization, Statistics play vital role in index selection.

    d. Statistics Provide information used to estimate I/O COST of the Index use.

    e. I/O Cost is expressed in terms of number of Logical page reads needed for the retrieval of Data.

    f. SQL SERVER do the Logical translates into Physical Read if required page is not available in memory cache.

Clustered Index vs. Non-Clustered Index

    a. Clustered Index contains the data pages at the leaf node.
    b. Non-Clustered index contains value and reference pointer to the data page.

    c. As Clustered index is created:

    d. Table pages are physically rearranged and resorted in the form of a B-tree. Therefore only one clustered index is possible for a table.

    e. All Non-Clustered indexes gets change-page reference is replaced with clustered index value for the leaf node containing data pages.
    f. Every Non-Clustered index contains Clustered index value at the leaf level.

Choosing useful indices

    a. Choosing a useful and appropriate index is very important for query Optimization.

    b. Index is useful when its I/O cost is less than I/O cost of a table scan.

    c. Index should be Highly Selective.

    d. Selectivity is measured opposite to density.

    e. Density=1/Cardinality of index (Number of index value that are present in the index data).

    f. How to choose index: that match your access pattern

g. Identify most commonly used SARG-able clause and then use them with an index.

Indices for Join Condition

a. Tables to be joined (or subsets which have been already restricted with some condition given in the where clause) are called the Join inputs

b. Three Types of Joins Operations:

c. Nested Loop are used when one table has less numbers of rows as compared to other join input. Extremely effective they require the least I/O and the fewest comparisons.

d. Merge Joins are used when both the inputs are approximately of same size. Merge joins requires presorted data and therefore it should be use only when this condition fulfills.

e. Hash Joins can process large, unsorted, non-indexed data effectively. It is the slowest way.

f. Primary Key, UNIQUE Constraints, Foreign Key are the mostly used for Joins.

g. BEST PRACTICE: index which are used in SARG-able clause can also be used for Joins.

Avoid Over Indexing

a. Avoid Creating Too many indexes.
b. Whenever data changes, index will also get change.
c. B-tree needs to be rebuilt again.
d. It Affects INSERT and UPDATE performance.
e. Create index that cover SARG-able WHERE clauses and Joins
f. Extend existing indexes to cover only for the queries that are slow and bookmark lookup because it carries most of the cost.
g. Do not create separate indexes for different purposes.

Other Techniques

Caching Data in the Application

a. Caching Data in the Application: It is a technique of keeping data in memory.

b. It reduces the number of reads from the database.

c. What can be cached:

> Data that changes very infrequently.

> Data that is expected to be used again in the future very shortly after it has been retrieved for the first time.

> Other design Considerations

  > Memory usage should be increase

  > Whenever the cached data changes at the source side notification should be provided.

  > Thread Protection.

Updates in Block

a. Bulk update and bulk delete operation can be broken into smaller blocks and try to keep the batch size to less than 50,000 records so that Lock escalation can be avoided.

b. Pros

> It helps in shortening the transaction duration.

> It also helps in reducing the Log file growth.

> It also Improves Locking problem by avoiding lock escalation from occurring.

c. Cons

> No transaction log for the entire operation

> What to do if one of the blocks fail?

> This technique is useful for conversations and batch jobs.

Improving Performance of queries

Use of proper Index

Clustered or non-clustered index can be created on column (s) to improve the performance of a query.

Guidelines for creating clustered index:

a. Clustered index is preferable on a table that is involved in less frequent inserts or updates
b. Clustered index should be created if column (s) are used frequently in GROUP BY, WHERE, ORDER BY clauses in queries.
c. If queries return range of values
d. If columns contain more unique values
e. If queries return large result set

Guidelines for creating non clustered index:

a. Non Clustered index is preferable on a table that is involved in more frequent inserts or updates
b. If column (s) are used frequently in WHERE clause in queries.
c. If queries return smaller result set
d. If columns contain lesser unique values

Index Fragmentation

Index creation is a onetime effort but rebuilding index needs to happen on a scheduled basis to persist the performance of searches as heavily fragmented index causes degradation in performance.

Number of days that would be required to rebuild index on a particular table would depend on frequency of searches and updates to the table.

The fragmentation % can be checked using

DBCC SHOWCONTIG
'Scan Density [Best Count: Actual Count]' parameter should be as close as 0%
'Logical Scan Fragmentation' parameter should be close to 100%
SQL Server 2008 and onwards, it's recommended to use sys.dm_db_index_physical_stats instead of SHOWCONTIG.

Depending on index fragmentation %, INDEX REORGANIZE or INDEX REBUILD (for % more than 30) should be done.

Analyzing execution plan

The execution plan can be seen using:
Query > Display Estimated Execution Plan – This will show the execution plan without executing the query
     Or

Query > Include Actual Execution Plan > Execute – This will first execute the query and then show the execution plan.

It can also be seen using SET SHOWPLAN statements

Once the plan is seen in Analyzer results window, following points can be checked for finding out issues:

a. Scan performed in the query execution – table scan or clustered index scan. Later is the more efficient one.
b. Less Efficient Plan – Query using less efficient plan is shown in RED.
c. Costly operation – Costly operation in a query can be identified looking at the cost shown below each operation and if a mouse is moved over the operation, estimated I/O or CPU cost can be seen.

Depending on the analysis of execution plan, step 2a, 2b or 2d onwards can be applied for performance improvements.

Guideline for writing queries:

a. Make sure that number of rows getting joined in a query are reduced by using conditions in WHERE clause to avoid query taking more time to execute.
b. Using temporary variable when lesser number of rows is expected performs better over temporary tables.
c. Avoid using cursors for traversing one row at a time, rather include the logic in a single query to improve performance.
d. Use joins instead of using nested queries.
e. Rather than using HAVING, use WHERE clause to eliminate number of rows first before using GROUP BY clause.
f. Use LEFT JOIN rather than using NOT IN.
g. SELECT only required columns rather than using SELECT * FROM tbl.

SET NOCOUNT ON

For queries getting executed by application or jobs, setting this option will refrain the 'Number of rows affected' message.

Use of Hints

Use join, table or query hints in case optimizer does not choose to use a particular efficient join or index.

Use of Partitioning

Having large volume of data in a single table deteriorates the performance of SELECT as well as INSERTS and UPDATES.
Hence using suitable partitioning scheme (round robin, hash or range), data should be partitioned across multiple tables.

Use of multiple files and file groups

In order to see the more performance improvements due to Partitioning, partitions should be stored on different files and file groups. This would lead to requests going to different files at the same time, processing in parallel and reduced blocking and wait time.

Use of Indexed views

Indexed view is a good option, in case few tables are constantly joined to retrieve results. These views are automatically updated when data in respective tables get updated and hence it's less efficient in cases when frequent updates occur on tables that are a part of indexed views.

String manipulations

String manipulations through SQL server T-SQL statements deteriorates the performance of processing and hence string operations intensive code should be written in SQL CLR code.

Denormalized Tables

Database table Normalization is advised while designing the database schema but if set of tables are required to be joined to serve searches that take more time, it is preferable to create denormalized tables in this scenario.

Use of Varchar(MAX), NVarchar(MAX) and VarBinary(MAX)

Varchar(MAX), NVarchar(MAX) and VarBinary(MAX) data types in SQL Server 2005 allows to save upto 2GB in a single variable. It allows you to use these data types as stored procedure parameters & variables.
Hence TEXT or NTEXT should be avoided as these are available just for backward compatibility and will be deprecated in next versions.

Use of Stored Procedures

Creating stored procedures reduces the network traffic and improves performance as well since execution plan for the stored procedure is cache in the procedure cache in SQL server.

Use sp_executesql

While dealing with dynamic SQL, use sp_executesql rather than using EXEC as there is an opportunity of reusing the execution plan with sp_executesql.

Query Performance Tips

1. Queries have to be written for the application keeping in mind the following things

    a. Avoid using string columns in joins between tables – use numeric columns as much as possible
    b. Try to use PKs of tables in joins as much as possible
    c. Avoid using "select *" – instead name the exact columns required in the select query
    d. Use integer data type for TYPE and STATUS columns as query retrieval will be fast. Front-end developers should maintain key-value relationship between status/type values and their integer enumerators in the constants file and pass integers instead of string to search queries.

2. Non-clustered indexes should be created for queries which are having bad performance.

3. Whenever there were columns in the SELECT list or WHERE clause of search queries and a non-clustered index was being created, try to save these columns on the B-Tree itself by using the INCLUDE clause.

4. After writing the queries, the Actual and Estimated Execution plan of the queries should be analyzed in the SQL Server Query Analyzer. We should try to reduce the number of Index and Table Scans and try to convert them to Index Seek by creating indexes on required join columns. Also, post-index creation execution plans are analyzed to check if the created index is being used or not – else the index is dropped.

5. Try to keep a tab on the number of indexes on a table as high number of indexes means higher costs for insert and update statements.

6. Use CTEs in stored procedures and batch queries instead of temporary tables and derived tables as the scope of CTE is limited to the immediate next statement in the batch and hence reduces disk I/O.
Set NOCOUNT ON at the beginning of batches to improve SQL Performance

Indexes

Performance of SQL server largely depends on how the index is defined on the column of any table. Index are generally of two types: 1) Clustered index 2) Non-clustered

- Only one clustered index can create on a table and data rows are sorted. Leaf level contains the actual data
- More than 1 and maximum of 999 non-clustered can be defined in single table and data rows are not sorted. Leaf level contains pointers to the actual data.

Most of the time developer will not put more importance to create index specifically on any table because SQL server by default create clustered index on primary key. And non-clustered index need to be created manually as per data load. Now issue comes when these default settings are applied in production. It doesn't work out for long period of time because of workload in production as a result, SQL Server performance start degrading. So as time passes and data load increased on database then we have to rethink on the indexes strategies. So now recreating the indexes is not a simple or easy task. It is a bit complex task. Basically it is a three step process.

- Collect the workload: Get the current work load from database with current default indexes.
- Analysis Index as per workload: Realizes whether this current index is fine for this work load or not.
- Update Index: Now if the current index is not appropriate then update the index.

The first two tasks cannot be done manually so one needs to use some tool. Now take a case where in database we have thousands of tables, lots of store procedure and lots of transaction. Then it is not possible to go & analysis all and come up with index plan. So for above first two tasks, SQL Server provides us with two tools. First is "SQL Profiler" and second is "Tuning advisor". SQL Profiler helps to automate the collection of workload. While the Tuning Adviser takes the workload gather by the SQL Profiler and come up with the appropriate indexes.

Database Engine Tuning Advisor (DTA)

Introduction

Database Engine Tuning Advisor (DTA) is an efficient tool in Microsoft SQL Server which provides DBA's with suitable physical design selection while installing SQL server. DTA has a wider scope and enhanced usability than Index Tuning Wizard (ITW), in SQL Server 2000.DTA can improve the performance of SQL statements and can also be used to tune large workload of updates and queries which is a set of transact-SQL statements that execute against a database or databases that the user wants to tune to. After evaluating the workload the DTA, specifies the best physical design to reduce the workload cost and optimize the same. DTA can assist both beginners and advanced DBA users. The user need not know the internal structure of the database to use the DTA.

Features of DTA

DTA has many enhanced features that are absent in ITW. They are:

- Session based tuning: DTA provides session based tuning where, whenever a DTA is invoked; it is stored as a named session. MSDB database stores this input/output and also the tuning log and reports. Various tuning result can be compared using this information.

- Extensive reports and feedback: Processed set of analysis reports are obtained as the output from DTA. The output specifies the impact on the workload incase the DTA that is recommended is accepted. DTA also provides feedback to the users about the process of tuning using tuning log. User can receives the statements being ignored by DTA using the tuning log as the reasons are recorded in the log

- Powerful what-if analysis: DTA offers effective what-if analysis by performing analysis according to the input given to DTA by the user for a particular physical design and database. This physical design is not materialized as the analysis is performed.

- Enterprise-ready performance: DTA can be used to tune databases as large as hundreds of GB, schemas as large as thousands of tables, workloads as large as several million SQL statements. Tuning can be completed in a batch window as DTA can be invoked with a time bound; this makes it suitable to be used in production environments. SQL Server 2000 installation can also be tuned by DTA.

Generating DTA workload

To use DTA, a user must provide a database as well as a workload to tune. This can be done in one of the following ways:

- When the user wants to tune a set of SQL statements, say a query with multiple lines or a batch of queries, then user must select the set of statements and choose Database Tuning Advisor from the Tools menu.
- Use a file enclosing SQL statements that are disjointed using GO.
- Using customized XML input file, weights can be consigned to different statements on an individual basis. When certain queries are known to be more important than other like in CEO query, these weights can be used. Statements with higher weights are prioritized with higher speed of execution as DTA automatically favors such physical design
- SQL Server Profiler trace stored in a file or table can be used. DTA requires accurate information for tuning, so tuning template should be used as it captures the exact information.

For tuning a database(s) or table(s), the use must specify which databases or optionally which table within databases. Multiple database tuning can be performed by DTA. Users must note that DTA can perform tuning process on the databases that have at least owner privileges.

DTA usage scenarios

DTA can be effectively used in the following scenarios:

- Tuning a SQL Server installation
- Third-party tuning tool can use DTA as a helper
- Tuning workloads of queries and updates
- Production server can use DTA for tuning
- Dealing with storage space
- Analyzing the effect of recommended changes
- Online index creation management
- Troubleshooting the performance of problem queries
- Executing an experimental what-if analysis
- Integrating manageability necessities

To decide on an effective physical design, DTA internally uses the following steps:

1. DTA analysis the workload and forms clusters of tables and columns. DTA search is restricted to these tables and columns.
2. Candidate structures are merged to form single candidates that optimal for at least one statement in the input workload.
3. In consultation with the SQL Server query optimizer, DTA chooses a subset of the candidates in an effective and efficient manner. There are many algorithmic modules such as candidate assortment, enumeration, merging and table/column group restriction that define these steps.

To improve the scalability of the tuning process, DTA uses various techniques such as:

- Wrapping for large workloads
- Compact statistics design for large databases
- Lazy database schema assembling for large schemas

The following figure spots how DTA makes jobs such as iterative tuning easier by taking benefit of the fast that both input and output can be in XML. The obtained output can be altered by the user any number of times and fed to the DTA as input till the required recommendation is touched.

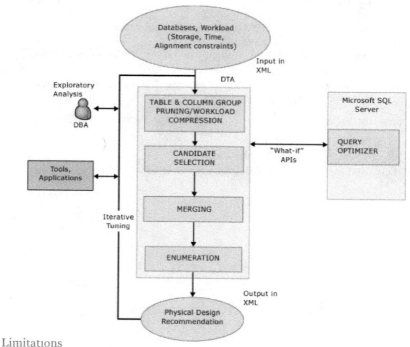

Limitations

DTA has few limitations, such as:

- DTA cannot be used to tune indexes in databases from Microsoft SQL Server 7.0.
- DTA cannot recommend indexes on system tables.
- DTA cannot tune single-user databases.
- DTA cannot tune a workload in a trace table that resides on a remote server(this is for security reasons)
- As DTA collects statistics by sampling the data, repeated sampling may result in different outputs.

- DTA cannot drop unique indexes or indexes that implement primary key or unique constraints.

www.ingramcontent.com/pod-product-compliance
Lightning Source LLC
Chambersburg PA
CBHW060936050326
40689CB00013B/3117